Great Customer Service Over The Telephone

By

The Customer Service Training Institute

Other Customer Service Training
Manuals from
The Customer Service Training Institute

Customer Service Basics

Service Recovery Skills

How to Interact with All Kinds of Customers

Enhancing the Customer Experience

Customer Service Training for Managers &
Supervisors

Customer Service Training for
Service Technicians

Customer Service Training for
the Hospitality Sector

Customer Service Training for
Health Care Professionals

Customer Service Excellence for
Security Officers

Safety in the
Workplace

"The telephone can be your greatest ally or your worst enemy. It all depends on how you use it!."

Table of Contents

Introduction

Ever since the telephone was first invented, it has been one of the most important and misused pieces of equipment in history. The telephone, when used properly, can be a huge resource and asset to any business. When used incorrectly, however, it can also be an instrument of frustration, anger, and customer dissatisfaction.

In this publication we will examine how we should use the telephone is different parts of our business and personal lives. We will discuss what to do and what not to do. We will look into ways to use the phone to communicate, create opportunity, and to increase sales.

We will also look into how the telephone has affected business and personal lives as technology has changed over the years and how we have evolved with this new technology. We will look at the benefits and the negatives associated with this change in technology and how to effectively use the phone properly.

Now, before we start, turn off your cell phone, put the office phone on "away" and concentrate on what you're reading!

How the Phone Has

Changed With Technology

Turn on an old movie on TV and see people in the old west turned the crank on the side of the phone to reach the operator. Watch people in the forties and fifties use the old rotary dial phones. See people sitting at switchboards patching in calls from one phone to another.

Now fast forward to today and watch people talking on tiny cell phones. See them use their multi-line home phone systems complete with call forwarding, call waiting, and home voice mail. This is just a small part of the technology we have witnessed on the last few decades. Other changes will follow and we will have new features available that we now only dream of.

With these changes comes a change in lifestyle. Technology comes with a price. We can now carry cell phones with us wherever we go but we lose the ability to have time to ourselves and privacy when we need it.

We can use phones to increase sales but our accounts can contact us 24 hrs. a day 365 days a year. We can take calls I the car, at the market, or during our children's sporting events and graduations. We have the convenience but give up a certain quality of life and privacy, which we had in the past.

On the positive side cordless phones have allowed us greater flexibility and phone systems have allowed even the smallest of businesses to have s system that would have only been found in a large corporation 20 years ago. We now can place people o hold, talk to more than one person at a time, and be notified when we are on the phone and someone else calls you.

As features increase, so does the ability to use them in ways that do not necessarily properly serve or customers or other people. Phone etiquette, something not even thought of in the fifties and sixties, is now a critical part of every business training package. Phone etiquette helps us make sure we are using the phone properly so that we give the proper impression to the person on the other end of the phone.

What Is Different About Doing Business Over The Phone!

When we communicate with others in person we use several different skills and senses. We communicate using more than just words. In fact, most of what we communicate in person, only a small fraction of what we communicate is in the words we speak.

When we communicate in person, we use the following skills and senses:

Words – The actual conversation we have contains words and phrases that help us communicate our thoughts, ideas, and desires.

Tone - More important than the words we speak is the tone we use in speaking them. Our tone conveys our feelings and emotions at that time. The same words have different meanings when we talk them softly versus yelling them at someone.

Expression – In face-to-face communication our facial expressions are part of our communication. Facial expressions convey our feelings and emotions at that particular time. Frustration, anger, happiness, etc. are all easily communicated via facial expressions.

Body Language- Body language is the way we stand or position ourselves during the conversation. People read different things into our body language. Crossing your arms during conversation, for example, is often viewed as being closed minded and unresponsive to ideas and thoughts. Getting too close to someone may make the other person uncomfortable and interfere with the conversation.

Actions - In person, some people use their arms, hands, and other parts of their body to emphasize things in the conversation. They may use their hands to represent the size or shape of something, or they may use them to describe a particular object or motion. Usually, the more emotional the individual becomes, the more they will resort to using their arms and hands to emphasize what they are saying at that time.

Appearance – When we communicate face-to-face, we often take into account the appearance of the person we are talking to. This is an important part of communication. Like it or not, people have their own perception of what an acceptable appearance is for a particular occupation or career.

For example, if someone was giving you advice on whether or not to have surgery, and that person was dressed in old dirty jeans, a torn shirt, and a three day beard, you would most likely dismiss his opinions if you knew little about him. He may be the premier authority in that particular field, but his appearance is not what you believe is proper and inspires little confidence. While this is sometimes unfair, it is a fact of life that we have these views and need to acknowledge them and deal with them.

Environment – The environment in which we communicate with others has an effect on how we communicate with each other. If it is a loud environment, we may need to raise our voices, which may give the wrong impression to our partner and cause our words to have the wrong meaning.

As you can see, there are many factors that help, or hinder, us in our attempts to effectively communicate with others. In order to be effective, we must make efforts to address all of these factors and learn how to use them to help you communicate properly.

First and foremost, the telephone is a device used for communication. We use it for keeping in touch with family and friends, do business, report emergencies, and countless other tasks. Most of the time we do all of this without even thinking about what we are doing.

We have all been brought up using the phone and have been taught by our families how we should use the phone.

Communicating over the phone is different than talking in person, as we have already discussed. Because of this, we have to learn how to get the information we need by using just words. We have to know what questions to ask, how and when to ask them, and how to guide the conversation in the right direction. Failure to accomplish this will result in customer frustration and dissatisfaction.

Think about something as simple as replacing a broken dinner plate. In person we would just take the plate to the store, match it up with the units on display, and pick out the correct plate to replace it. Sounds simple enough. So simple that often the customer does this all on their own.

One the phone, however, this is a totally different process. Think about all you have to know to figure out which plate to ship to the customer. What questions will you need to ask? You may have to know:

What size is the plate?

What color is it?

Does it have a design?

If so, what kind of design is it?

What color is the design?

How old is the plate?

Does it have a manufacturer stamped on the back?

Does it have any trim on the plate? If so, what color is the trim?

Etc. etc. etc.

If you fail to ask all the necessary questions, you run the risk of sending the customer the wrong plate. Then you will have to arrange for the return of the plate, which results in more inconvenience for the customer, which reduces customer satisfaction.

Getting information over the phone usually requires a more thorough level of product knowledge than face-to-face conversation. You need to know what information is needed to make an accurate decision. You need to know all the different variations of a product and when those products were produced. You need to know everything about a product to make the correct decision.

Don't be afraid to ask questions. Sometimes you will have to ask a lot of them. If a customer starts to get impatient, try to explain to them that there are a lot of possible products out there and a little time spent now will save a lot of inconvenience later. Most people will be receptive to this approach.

Try and view every phone contact as a puzzle. Some puzzles will be easy. Transferring a caller to the person they ask for is easy. Transferring a caller to the correct person for a particular task might be a little harder. Dealing with an unusual request may be tougher yet.

Questions are wonderful tools for any kind of problem solving situation. Phone conversations generally require more of them because we cant use our eyes and other senses to help us.

The good news is that the longer you do the job the easier it becomes. Can you remember your first day on any job? You had a hard time doing even the simplest task because you were not familiar with anything! The second day was a little easier and by the end of the first week you were starting to feel a little comfortable. The same goes with using the phone. Once you get comfortable with using the system and talking with people, the easier things get. Once you get familiar with your products or services, the easier it will be to answer questions.

Once we experience something, we file little bits of information about it in our mind. The next time the situation comes up, we remember a little of what we did to resolve it. The more situations we experience, the more comfortable and at ease we become.

When communicating over the phone do not take anything for granted. Ask however many questions are needed to either resolve a problem or complete a task.

If you are asked to transfer someone to another person to resolve an issue, make sure you find out what the issue is so you know the right person to transfer to.

Last but certainly not least, if you don't know the answer to a particular question, ask someone who does know the right answer! Don't try to bluff your way through it or try and make an educated guess. Ask the questions and listen to the answers before making any decisions.

Communicating Over the Phone

When we communicate over the phone, we have an entirely different set of factors that affect us. We have discussed the need to ask questions, now let's understand why.

Over the phone, we cannot see whom we are talking to. That means that body language and appearance have little to do with our communication. Body language still plays a small part because the body language of the parties involved will help them convey their emotions at that time. If a person is angry, their body language will represent that feeling and help strengthen or prolong that feeling. By and large, however, we will be dealing with the following factors when talking over the phone:

Words – When talking over the phone, words play a greatly increased role in our communication. We do not have the ability to use our hands to demonstrate things or make our point.

Tone - The tone we use over the phone helps convey how we feel at that moment. Frustration, anger, and even helplessness, are all represented in our voices during conversation. This comes across very clearly over the phone.

Environment – The environment in which all parties are in is also important over the phone. We must be in an environment that allows us to easily hear what all parties are saying. Without being easy to hear people over the phone, a certain level of frustration may appear. Cell phones, present a different challenge, as some phones do not allow you to listen and talk at the same time. Very often words are cut off by outside noises and other factors.

Helplessness - Always keep in mind that, when someone calls you on the phone, they are relying on you to address their needs or to get them to the correct person for their needs. The caller has no ability to walk over to someone else, try to find another person that knows what to do, etc. You are their sole contact and you must know what to do, when to do it, and how to do it. This feeling may make your caller a little nervous, helpless, and, if they had problems in the recent past, frustration.

When talking over the phone, we must relay on the words we hear and the emotions behind them. Very often, the emotions behind the words are more important than the words themselves.

In order to communicate effectively, we must:

Take control over the entire phone experience from the beginning to the end.

Make the entire process seamless and easy for those who call you.

Learn to listen and communicate properly so your customer's needs are properly addressed.

Knowing How The System Works!

This may seem to be just common sense but the person on the phone needs to know how their phone system works! From a simple one-line home phone to a huge multi-line commercial system, you need to know how to properly use it!

Even small home phones today have features that were only available on expensive commercial systems in the past. These features are useless if you don't know how to use them. Always keep in mind that any mistake you make on the phone can result in a lost or "dropped" call. When this happens, your caller must start at the very beginning and will tend to be somewhat annoyed although understanding.

While every system is different and will not have every feature other systems may have, it is important that you know how to perform the basic tasks that you will be expected to perform on a daily basis.

Some of these tasks are listed below but your particular job may require additional tasks that you should learn.

Answer calls

Transfer calls

Place calls on hold

Use voicemail

Page employees

Answering calls-   Perhaps the most basic of all skills, you need to know how to identify which line is ringing and how to properly answer the call. Without being able to answer the call, you can' do anything else.

Transferring calls- Most of the time, you will not be the only source of information available to the caller. Not only that, but you cannot be expected to be an expert on every aspect of your company's business. Because of this, you need to know how to transfer your caller to the correct individual without losing the call. Failure to complete this task makes the caller have to start all over from the beginning and may result in that caller going elsewhere for their business!

Placing calls on hold – Very often you will have multiple lines ringing, or will have to ask the caller to hold while you get them the information they have requested. When this happens, you will want to place the customer on hold. This is more effective and professional than just placing the receiver down. Placing a caller on hold allows you to talk and carry out business without the caller hearing you on the other end of the phone. We will talk more on this later.

Using voicemail – A callers phone call is important and you do not want to lose the reason that made the caller phone you in the first place. Also, there may be an instance where the person you want to transfer the caller is not available. When these situations occur, you will need to know how to use the voicemail system. It is far better to give the caller an option to leave a message rather than ask them to call back later. Every caller should be thought of as a potential sale or customer lead.

Using the paging system- Some companies use a paging system to locate employees whose jobs require them to roam from place to place. When these people are needed, you either page them using an overhead PA system or page them on their pager. When you need to contact these individuals you need to know how to do this.

These are just some of the most basic and common features and tasks that you will need to learn and use daily. There may be additional tasks you will need to learn for your particular position or system. It is important that you take the time to learn everything you will need to do before you are actually on the job and handling callers. You need to practice with co-workers and friends rather than on actual callers.

If you are expected to start handling actual callers without any training, try and practice on a friend, spouse, or co-worker. Even if it is just a few minutes at the start of your day, try and practice before fielding actual calls. It will be well worth your while.

The Importance of the First Contact

In many businesses, answering the phone is done without much thought or preparation. There is not much importance attached to it at all. This is a huge mistake!

When someone calls you or your company, how they are greeted and talked to over the phone determines what initial impression the caller has of the company. If the greeting is friendly and professional, the caller will begin to form a favorable and positive opinion of the company. If the greeting is rough and crude in nature, the caller will begin to form a negative opinion of the company.

Initial opinions and feelings are important as the entire process that will follow is determined by our initial feelings. We as human beings take all information available to us when we make judgments and decisions.

These judgments are based on our experiences, what we are taught, and our environment. These opinions are very strong and tend to influence how we react in a particular situation

When we go into a store, doctor's office, or other location, we see the surroundings, feel the atmosphere, smell the odors, and many other things that help us form judgment and opinions. If all this information seems appropriate to us then we will begin to feel comfortable with the operation and develop positive feelings. If things seem not appropriate, a negative opinion will follow.

The key here is appropriate. What we see and hear must be appropriate. You can't make a general statement such as; "For me to feel comfortable, everything must be clean." While this certainly would hold true for a doctor's office, it would not necessarily be true for an auto shop or a junkyard. For us to feel good about a pace, we must experience what we think we should experience.

When we talk to someone over the phone, we do not have the benefit of seeing things firsthand. We cannot see product displays, immaculately clean offices, or smell the wonderful smell of fresh bread at a bakery. All we have to go by is what we hear over the phone. While it is just words, we also process several bits of information contained in those words.

Tone of Voice

It would surprise most of us to know that the words we use represent only a fraction of what we hear. While the words convey a message we want to send, the way we speak these words is often more powerful than the words themselves. How we speak them may mean the difference between conveying the intended message or something completely different.

When we talk to anyone over the phone we should always use a calm and controlled voice. It should be free of tension, be pleasant to hear, and be a calming presence on the phone. We should not appear to be rushed, stressed, or convey any emotion other than a sincere desire to help whomever has called us.

If we are tense and rushed on the phone these emotions are picked up by the caller and may tend to make the caller feel the same way too. When this happens the chances of a truly positive experience go down significantly. When one or more people do not feel comfortable, the chances of getting the correct information and forming a positive opinion are greatly reduced.

What happens when you call someone and they answer the phone very roughly and abrupt? Does that make you feel good or does it make you feel a little frustrated and skeptical about the person or company that you have called?

Does that kind of greeting inspire confidence or skepticism? Do you develop positive or negative opinions about the person or the business?

If you are like the vast majority of people, you will form negative opinions when exposed to this kind of treatment over the phone. People respond positively to positive words, pleasant voice tone, and a calming presence. This is what you need to present to every caller.

Emotion

Your emotions are readily recognized in your voice. If you are angry, your voice will convey this anger. The exact opposite will happen if you are very happy. When you are in a good mood, or very happy, your voice will convey that to the other person and the conversation will take on a more relaxed tone.

It is often said that it takes more than one person to make an argument. That is always not true but it does take more than one person to sustain and argument. An angry customer is going to start to argue but it is how the other parties respond that often dictates whether the argument will continue or whether the situation will calm down and some real, meaningful dialog can begin to take place.

Positive vs. Negative Words

One way to create a positive atmosphere during a conversation is to avoid the use of negative sounding words.

Words such as can't, won't, no, shouldn't, and not convey a negative feeling that will often cause the other person to stop listening to what you are saying. As soon as they hear the negative word their minds shut down all hearing and they begin to formulate their response to your refusal. Even if you follow a negative response with a positive response, it is possible that the other person may not even hear the positive part of your statement.

People react negatively towards a negative comment and positively to a positive comment. Anything that makes another person happy or receptive should be used during a conversation.

Background Noise

In order for someone to understand what you are saying, they have to be able to hear you speak. If you are talking with loud noises in the background, your voice is going to be hard to understand and the other party may just give up trying to understand you. If at all possible, try to conduct all phone conversations in an area that is fairly quiet and free from outside distractions.

In order to be effective on the phone, or even in person, you need to make every effort to make it as easy as possible to carry on a conversation with you. That would mean you should speak clearly and not too fast, have a minimum of distractions around you, and be able to speak in such a manner that the other parties involved can follow and understand you.

Proper Phone Presence

NOTE: This chapter may be a little offensive to some people. Please do not take the information provided within to be prejudicial in nature or as an excuse to make judgments based on a person's race, color, or creed.

It is important for businesses to develop the right employees for positions involving a considerable amount of phone contact. The people chosen must be able to communicate easily and effectively with the majority of those people who call in for assistance. To make sure this is accomplished, a business needs to fully understand their customer base and their individual needs.

For example, if your company does business in an area that has a large Spanish population and a large English speaking population, then the people in charge of answering the phones should be able to speak both Spanish and English. If this is not possible, then an electronic system asking prospective callers which language they prefer should be used.

There are a lot of companies that deal with people in several countries. In these cases, maybe there are 5 or 6 languages involved. Since most people do not speak all these different languages, then the automated system works well for directing callers to the correct person for the rest of the call.

Just speaking the language, however, is often not enough. In order to be effective over the phone, we must be able to speak the required language in such a way that we can be easily understood. This may mean that people who speak a language but do so with a very heavy or hard to understand accent, may not be a good choice for this type of position. We are not talking about discrimination here but rather a person's ability to fulfill the responsibilities of a particular position.

We have talked about the need to be able to be easily understood. Whenever a person is not easy to understand we place a burden on the other party to try and make sense out of something they may not understand. This often leads to confusion, frustration, and tension. This is exactly what we want to avoid.

I think it is important that, when we interview candidates for positions involving heavy phone contact, we actually conduct part of the interview on the phone. This way we can ask questions and see how the candidate communicates over the phone.

Is he or she easy to understand? Can they communicate effectively over the phone without requiring an above average effort by the other parties? If the voice pleasant and inspire a positive dialog? All of these things should be part of any interview process for positions involving heavy customer contact.

Keep in mind that we only have words and sound to convey our message over the phone. While some people can use hand gestures, body motions, and other ways to get their point across in person, you cannot do this over the phone. This may seem like common sense but you can't see movement on a phone.

Sometimes businesses hire very attractive people to act as receptionists. Their appearance may be key to the business they are representing such as a very well built person representing a gym or fitness center. Perhaps a very attractive woman representing a spa or beauty salon would be appropriate. While this is important on some situations, it is important to realize that appearance counts for exactly nothing when talking on the phone. People don't know if you're short or tall, overweight or thing, and bald or hairy over the phone. What they get is the voice, that's it!

The key attributes to those people who are responsible for heavy phone contact are:

Pleasant sounding voice that puts people at ease.

A calm personality that will reduce tension and reduce problems.

A voice that is easy to understand but a majority of your customers.

An ability to think rationally and follow instructions.

The ability to resolve problems and diffuse issues.

When the correct person is put in this position, everyone in the company, and all the customers, reap the benefits. The benefits are happier customers, reduced stress, and a more pleasant "flow" when using the telephone within the company.

How Personal Should You Make It?

Whenever we talk on the phone, there are different levels of intimacy between the people talking. The conversation could be very proper and professional or very informal and personal. It is up to you to determine which approach is proper under the circumstances.

The circumstances surrounding the conversation will determine what type of conversation it will be. Another determining factor would be the type of business or industry you are in. For example, a receptionist in a lawyer's office would answer the phone differently than a receptionist in a beauty salon.

Generally speaking we take our lead by what is considered acceptable within our industry. We would take into consideration what or customers would expect and act accordingly. Always keep in mind that we should provide our customers with the type of experience they expect or better.

We should never give any caller or customer a feeling that our conduct or representation is improper.

Perhaps the most important detail we need to think about is how formal we should be when taking to a caller. Do we want to talk to callers on a first name basis or a full name basis? Whatever your decision is, your greeting should take the lead and set up the expectation of the conversation to follow. You would then take the customers lead as to how to follow. For example:

You: Good afternoon, thank you for calling Lewis & Son, attorney at law. This is Anne. How may I help you?

Caller: Hello. This is Mrs. Lasher. May I speak to Mr. Lewis?

In this example you set up the flow in your greeting that it is all right to be on a first name basis with the caller. The caller's reply indicates, however, that she wishes to be on a full name basis. She introduced herself as Mrs. Lasher. She did not say, this is Christine Lasher. If she introduced herself as Christine Lasher, then it would be appropriate to continue on a first name basis. Let's continue the above conversation in two ways:

First Name Basis:

You: "Hello Mrs. Lasher. This is Anne. Mr. Lewis is not available right now.

Is there something I can help you with?

Caller: "Hello Ann. Please call me Christine. I just needed to know when I will be receiving the contract in the mail. We have a closing next week."

You: "I can find out when Mr. Lewis is done with his meeting and then I'll call you back. Would that be all right, Christine?"

Full Name Basis

You: "Hello, Mrs. Lasher. This is Ann. Mr. Lewis is not available right now. Is there something I can help you with?"

Caller: "I need to know when I will be receiving the contract in the mail. Could you please have him call Mrs. Lasher?"

You: "I can find out when Mr. Lewis is done with his meeting and then I'll call you back. Would that be all right Mrs. Lasher?"

In the first example, the caller clearly instructed you to use her first name during the conversation. In the second, the caller still used her full name (or used Mr. or Mrs.) in the conversation. When this happens, you should continue to use the full name of the caller in future conversations until you are told to use just a first name.

Very often a caller will start out with a somewhat formal conversation until he or she becomes a little more comfortable with you and your company. As the comfort level increases, they may switch over to a less formal manner. Whatever the caller wants you should do your best to respect.

Some people are not comfortable at all with first name basis conversations. They feel it is an intrusion on the "space" and further attempts to develop a first name based conversation will not be productive. This feeling may be based in culture or religion. It may be just a personal preference. Whatever the reason, you should respect the caller and talk to him in such a manner that makes he or she comfortable and at ease.

Another aspect of conversation we need to address is the degree of formality we use when talking over the phone. While personal conversations between family and friends are very informal, this is usually not acceptable in business.

In business, we need to maintain a level of professionalism and respect with each caller. The level of professionalism we use should also be appropriate for the business or industry we are working in. The greeting we use should be appropriate and inspire confidence in the minds of our callers. After that, each conversation will be treated individually.

Generally speaking, professional offices such as doctors and lawyers will use more formal formats in dealing with callers.

This is strictly because this is what is expected in those situations. It is a reflection on the office and type of service provided and is designed to inspire confidence and impart a certain level of professionalism.

For example, you would not be impressed if you called a criminal law office and the receptionist answered the phone like this:

Reception: "Hello, you've reached Lewis &Son. The is Annie. What can I do for ya?"

Caller: "This is Mr. Miller. Can I speak with Mr. Lewis, please?"

Receptionist: "Hey, dude. Mr. Lewis isn't here. Don't know when he'll be back either. Why don't you call back around 3 PM?"

I doubt if you would feel comfortable in dealing with this law firm in the future. This is because you now have an impression of inappropriate conduct and a poor impression of the firm based on the receptionist's manner over the phone. This is because how he or she spoke over the phone was inappropriate for the situation.

If you were to take the same exact conversation and used in for a record store, tattoo parlor, or a youth oriented business, then everything may be just fine and no offense would be taken.

That is because the conversation is deemed appropriate for the surrounding circumstances.

You could relate this to a first impression made in person. If you met a lawyer dressed in dirty jeans and a t-shirt, you would not feel impressed or confident. The same would go for an auto mechanic who came out of the garage in a 3-piece suit. Switch the two people and everything would be fine. Again, it is all about being appropriate and acting appropriately in a situation.

There will be times when you are unsure how to proceed. When this occurs, it is better to proceed on the more formal side and take your lead from the caller. Do not drastically change your approach but rather gradually switch over to either more or less formal, as caller wants.

It is also a good idea for everyone in a company to use the same type of demeanor on the phone. All reception people should use the same level of formality so that the experience is uniform for every caller. An opinion or impression of a person or business is formed over several interactions with the office. If a caller gets several different types of treatment from different people, then their impression may be one of confusion rather than one of security.

As in everything else in business, we should make every effort to create an environment that is stable, uniform, and appropriate to our callers or customers. To help achieve this, we need to make sure that everyone is instructed how to interact with callers.

We often train salespeople and retail clerks on how to interact with customers, why should telephone conversations be treated differently.

One effective way to achieve this is to make up a "telephone handbook" which would be used as a resource for both new and existing employees. This manual would list items such as required greetings, formality requirements, as well as transfer procedures and other telephone matters. This manual would then be used to provide a constant resource to insure uniform treatment no matter which person should answer the phone.

Automated Phone Systems

One of the most profound impacts of technology in telephone systems has been the arrival of the automated phone system. An automated phone system is a system that electronically answers the phone and provides a list of options for the caller to choose. Based on the caller's entry on their touch-tone keypad, the system then directs the call to a pre-programmed destination.

The main advantage of this kind of system for businesses is that they do not require an actual person to answer the phone, which saves them money. Another advantage is that the system reacts to the same request the exact same way every time, which eliminates human error.

A disadvantage of these kinds of systems is that customers either dislike them or downright hate them!

Customers view these systems as impersonal and feel like they are being treated as a machine themselves!

Usually these systems are used to direct callers to a particular department where the phone will be answered by a real person. For example, the system may say; "Please press 1 for sales, 2 for service, or 3 for our billing department" This kind of response is well received by customers because it gets them were they need to go quickly and easily. That is a benefit in the eyes of the customer.

Here is the system that customers hate:

"Please press 1 for sales or 2 for service"
You press 1
"Please press 1 for US sales or 2 for foreign sales"　　　You press 1

"Please press 1 for commercial sales or 2 for retail sales"　　You press 2

"Please press 1 for equipment sales and 2 for service sales"　　　You press 1

"Please press 1 for power tools and 2 for hand tools"　　　　　You press 1

"Please press 1 for cordless tools or 2 for corded tools"　　You press 1

"For our heavy duty cordless press 1 for others press 2"　You press 1

"For cordless saws press 1 for cordless drills press 2"   You press 1

"For cordless jig saws press 1 for circular saws press 2"   You press 2

"For trim saws press 1 for all other saws press 2,"   You press 2

"To locate a dealer in your area press 1 otherwise press 2"   You press 2

"To request a product catalog press 1 otherwise press 2"   You press 2

"To leave a message press 1 to speak to an operator press 2"You press 2

"I'm sorry the line is busy. Please leave a message or try again later."

"Thank you. Goodbye"

Systems that provide too many levels of questions and options create confusion and frustration in customers. If they miss a question, very often they find it impossible to go back. If they answer something wrong by mistake, sometimes they must start over at the beginning. This is not good for the business or the customer.

It is a good practice to design a system that has a limited number of questions and an easy way to get back to the last question or the beginning from any point in the process.

It is also desirable to have the option available at any time to speak to a live person. This enables the caller to exit the system at any time when they get to a point where they need to do that.

Automated systems enable businesses to handle more calls with fewer people. When used correctly they help speed up service and increase the speed at which things get done. Many businesses, however, take these systems and make them too hard to navigate or too long and complicated to use. When this occurs, the negatives far outweigh the benefits for the company.

In order to have a well-received system, the system should be:

- Be easy to use and understand.
- Have a limited number of levels for a caller to go through.
- Able to give the option of speaking to a real person at any time.
- Able to go back to the previous level or to the beginning.
- Provide accurate responses and good service to the customers

Most of the voices used in these systems are the same electronic voice. If you have the option of using your own voice on the system, please make sure that this voice is friendly and pleasant to listen to. It must be easy to understand with minimal effort. Always keep in mind that an electronic system does not allow a customer to have anything repeated to them if they don't hear correctly. They may go back to the menu but each response is a "canned response" and cannot be changed if someone does not understand it. Because of this, it is critical that everything be extremely easy to understand.

Using Speakerphones

Let's take a moment to talk about speakerphones. Speakerphones are devices that use a speaker instead of a handset to speak and talk through. The advantage of a speakerphone is that more than one person can hear and talk at the same time. In fact, a large group of people can simultaneously participate in a conversation via speakerphone.

There should be a certain degree of etiquette involved in the use of speakerphones, however.

If you are the one who wants to use the speakerphone so more people can hear the conversation, you should make the other people involved aware that you are placing the call on the speakerphone. This is done to make sure the other party is aware that their comments are no longer private.

When using a speakerphone, anyone within earshot of the phone can hear what is being said. In cases where comments are made that are not intended for certain individuals, saying these comments over a speakerphone would be a disaster.

It is not considered out of place to ask if the call is on a speakerphone. While this does not guarantee an honest answer, it does provide a clear indication that one party does not want the call to be on speakerphone for whatever reason. This gives a warning to all concerned that speakerphone use should be discontinued.

If you are the one that is using the speakerphone, you should state to all involved that you are using a speakerphone and ask if there are any objections. This just shows your respect for the others involved.

There are different types of speakerphone systems. The less expensive systems only allow one-way conversations at a time. This means that one phone is in talk mode and the other is in listening mode. Sometimes this is awkward and results in lost words or comments. As the conversation starts, you will quickly notice if you are dealing with this kind of system. Be aware of his and plan your comments accordingly.

Other systems operate just like regular phones. You can talk and listen at the same time. When using these types of systems you can talk and listen just like normal. Always be aware of the system you are using and plan accordingly.

Another important consideration is the sound quality involved with using a speakerphone. Here are some of the factors that may affect the conversation when using a speakerphone:

Sound quality – Using a speakerphone usually involves a loss in sound quality.

Background noise – Any kind of noise in the background will be picked up by the speakerphone and become part of the conversation.

System type – one or two-way conversation capability is a major consideration on whether or not you should use a speakerphone.

Privacy – the free exchange of ideas and comments may be impaired when using a speakerphone. When a person is unsure about who is listening they may be less than forthright regarding what they say.

There are a few situations where speakerphones are very desirable. The most common reasons are:

Whenever there are several people or large groups that wish to participate in the conversation or listen to the caller.

When one or more of the participants wants to work hands free. One person may want to listen to data and fill in a wall chart at the same time for example.

If it is desired to record the conversation a speakerphone makes it easy to record all parts of the conversation as it happens.

In short, speakerphones present us with unique benefits but require special consideration as to the correct way to use them. Remember that the privacy of everyone involved is sacrificed when a speakerphone is being used.

Under no circumstances should confidential or delicate information be transmitted over a speakerphone. If this kind of information needs to be given then the call should be taken off speakerphone, the information given in private, and then the call placed back on speakerphone. This reduces the information from being heard by anyone who happened to listen in at that point in the conversation.

Answering The Phone

One of the things we have always been taught since we were small children is to be polite and make a good first impression. We were taught that when we meet or talk to someone for the first time, it is important to act and speak properly. Why do you think this is important?

The first time we talk to someone on the phone, or meet them in person, both parties know nothing about the other except for what they have heard from others about you. Because of this, the person's mind will be open to forming an honest opinion about you. From this point on, how you treat the caller will determine what he or she feels about you and the company your represent.

The funny thing about this is that you only have this opportunity once! The next time you speak to this individual they are going to remember who they were treated during the last conversation.

Therefore, they will either have a positive or negative feeling about you before you even pick up the phone. This is called "emotional baggage" which means emotions and thoughts left over from previous experiences.

Because you only get one chance to make a first impression, I strongly urge everyone who is involved in heavy phone contact to treat every conversation like it is a first time contact. Since you never know who is on the other end of the phone (unless you have caller ID), you should always be on your "best behavior" and treat everyone the very best you can.

Your Greeting!

At home you answer the phone usually by just saying "hello?" This is acceptable because it is a social environment and formality is not required or expected. In a business environment, however, this type of greeting falls way short of what is required to make a good impression for you and your company.

First, your greeting should be friendly sounded and "upbeat" in tone. It should inspire confidence and start to put the caller at ease. If you answer the phone in a rough and abrupt manner, you will tend to place the caller on the defensive as if he or she expects an argument to follow. It should also thank the caller for calling your business.

Second, your greeting should tell the caller what business or store he has reached. This lets your caller confirm that he has reached the number that he wants. Without this information the caller may start talking to someone at a different place than he intended to call!

An example would be; "Hello thank you for calling XYZ Corporation." Now the caller knows which company he has called and that the number he or she have is correct.

After identifying the company name, you should let the caller know whom they are talking to. Your first name is enough at this point. Giving a caller your name makes the call a little more personal and makes continuing the conversation a little easier. An example would be; "Hello, than you for calling XYZ Corporation. This is Eileen." Now the caller can refer to you by name. He also has a name of someone that he can refer to at a later date if the need arises.

Lastly, you need to ask a question in your greeting so you know how to proceed. Asking the question makes continuing the call less awkward than waiting for the caller to say what he is calling for. You may ask "How may I help you?, How may I direct your call?, or any other question that will help you decide what needs to be done at this point.

Putting all these pieces together will give you a greeting like: "Hello, thank you for calling XYZ Corporation. This is Eileen. How may I help you?" When spoken in the correct tone and voice, this is a highly effective way of answering the phone and establishing contact with a caller. It is short yet effective and let's the customer feel confident in both you and your company.

Designing a greeting will be up to the particular business involved. A law firm, for example, would have a different greeting than the local food market. No matter what the business, however, the greeting must be professional and establish a positive feeling in the mind of the caller.

One thing we do not want to do is answer the phone in a rough or crude manner. Answering the phone with a; "Yeah?" or "XYZ" does not inspire confidence and in fact, will make the caller feel like they are interrupting something and will not get the proper treatment from you or your company. A proper greeting only takes a few seconds and is very beneficial to all parties.

We do not, however, want to make the greeting too long or too full of information. This is just annoying and confusing to the customer and may sound like a commercial. Imagine if you called a company and the greeting was something like this: "Hello, than you for calling XYZ Corporation, home of the new XYZ 4000 the very best in home entertainment systems and in-home theatre systems. Our systems bring the movie theatre experience right into your living room with state of the art electronics all enclosed in sleek and beautiful enclosures. When you think of home theatres, think of XYZ. How may I help you?" Do you think your head would be about to explode after that greeting? What kind of mood do you thin you would be in at this point?

Your greeting should be easy to understand, include all the basic information described in these pages, and be friendly and upbeat. Depending on the business you're in, your greeting may be shorter or longer and include different options. Whatever your greeting may be, be sure that it is short and to the point while being professional and informative.

Always remember that your greeting sets the tone for the conversation that follows. By taking time to make a proper greeting, the rest of the process may go much smoother and get better results.

Transferring Callers

Transferring a caller to another party is a very important aspect of phone etiquette. There are specific things that should be done when transferring callers. These steps are as follows:

Listen to what the caller needs – Just as a doctor listens to symptoms to make their diagnosis, you need to listen to the caller, identify their needs, and decide what needs to be done.

Determine who can help the caller – After you have assessed their needs, determine what department or individual can help the caller resolve their problem, provide their information, etc.

Give the caller the name of that person and their department – Once you have determine who can help them, give the caller that person's name so they will know whom they are talking to. If that person is in another department, branch, etc., let them know that also. This way, if they get disconnected at some point, your caller will have the information to call back and ask for that person.

Give the caller that person's direct phone number if it exists. – Just as giving them the person's name helps them if they have to call back, giving them the new person's direct phone number (if the person has a direct number) will help them if they get disconnected, or if they need to call back with the same problem in the future.

Make the transfer yourself – Always transfer the caller to the person who can help them. NEVER tell the caller to call back and ask for that person. The only time that is acceptable is if you do not have the capability to transfer the caller yourself. It is good phone service to make the transfer yourself and make it easier on the caller.

Tell the caller you are transferring them to that person. – Before you transfer the caller, let them know what you are doing and why. This way the caller will know what's going on and will be able to understand what's happening every step of the way. Say; "Mrs. Smith, I am going to transfer you over to Mr. Jones in marketing. His direct extension is 2015 and he will be able to help you."

Make the transfer and stay on the line. – Make the transfer and stay on the line to make sure that the transfer goes through. If the person is not at his or her desk and the call goes through to voice mail, decide if there is someone else who can help.

If not, explain to the caller that the person is not there and that you will put them through to their voice mail. If the person is available, then proceed to the next step.

Introduce the caller to the new person and explain their problem. – When you transfer a caller to the new person, help prepare both parties with an introduction where you introduce both parties and briefly explain the issues involved. You would say something like; "Hello Mr. Jones, I have Mrs. Smith on the line and she has a problem with her widget. She wants to upgrade it and does not know how to proceed." This allows both parties to start on the same page and does not make the caller start from the beginning with the new person. This is particularly effective when there are specific terms and language that are used to describe issues and problems. Making sure the new person correctly understands what needs to be done makes chances of success improve greatly.

Say goodbye to the caller and thank them. – Close out your part of the call by thanking the customer and saying goodbye. Saying something like: "Mr. Jones will help you now Mrs. Smith, thank you for calling and have a good day.

The entire process is designed to take the caller by the hand throughout the entire process and keep them informed every step of the way. Think about how the caller feels.

They can't see what you are doing and there is a certain amount of helplessness being felt at this point. By explaining what you are doing, who you are transferring them to, and what their information is, you give the caller information they can use in the future and make them feel confident in what is going on.

Another reason for following this procedure is that it is absolutely foolproof. By keeping the caller informed, and handling the entire process you, you are making it easy on the caller and insuring that the process goes right. By staying on the line and making the introduction and providing the details, you insure that everything will go as planned. There may be a time when the person might say; "I don't handle that but Mr. Evans can help you." You can then make that transfer and get things going again. In cases like these, you would offer a small apology and begin the transfer process.

We want to make things as easy and seamless to the caller as possible. By following this procedure, we insure that our caller will have a pleasant experience that will impress them and leave them with positive feeling towards you and your company.

Putting Callers On Hold

Perhaps one of the most frustrating times for callers is when they are placed on hold. Callers might be put on hold for a number of reasons. Maybe there are too many people waiting to speak with someone, they are waiting for information, or the person they wish to speak to is not immediately available.

There are specific practices to follow when placing a caller on hold. They are as follows:

Ask the caller if you can place them on hold or offer to let them leave a message or voice mail. – Always ask the caller if it is all right to place them on hold. Give them whatever options that are available such as voice mail, leaving a message, etc. If no options are available, always give the option of calling back even though this is not a good option in any circumstance.

Give them an approximate wait time. – One thing callers absolutely hate is being placed on hold for long periods of time. It is only fair to let the customer know how many callers are ahead of them or the expected amount of time the caller can expect to be on hold. With this information, the caller may elect to leave a message, stay on the line, or call back later. In any case, the caller is aware of the expected wait time and will not be unpleasantly surprised.

Check back with the caller periodically to make sure the customer knows they are still connected. – When customers are placed on hold for more than a minute or so, try and check back every 2 or 3 minutes to let them know that they are still on hold and have not been disconnected. Sometimes music on hold will help this and some systems have automatic messages that do this for you.

Thank the caller for their patience. – If you do make contact with the customer prior to them coming off of hold, thank them for their patience and then forward them to their destination.

Let them know when the person is available and connect them. – Let the customer know that you care going to connect them and then make the transfer.

One very important thing to remember is that being placed on hold is a very frustrating and unproductive time for the caller.

Usually, when callers are placed on hold, they are not doing anything else while they wait. They may have the TV on or radio, but mostly the time on hold is unproductive time and keeps the caller from accomplishing other things.

Take a moment and look at your watch. If you have a timer, set it for one minute and just sit with your eyes closed. Do nothing for this minute. Just sit and concentrate on the time.

Do you see how long just one minute can seem like when you are on hold? Imagine doing the same thing for 5, 10, or 15 minutes! The fact is, the longer a person is placed on hold, the less chance you have of making that caller satisfied with the call. You must make every effort to minimize wait time for these callers.

To reduce frustration for your callers, you may want to use one of the following alternatives:

Offer a phone call back – Offer your caller a call back from the person within a defined timeframe. Saying something like; "Mr. Smith is not available right now and it looks like it will be a bit of a wait. Would you like him to call you back by the end of business today?" gives the caller an option instead of waiting on the phone or calling. When doing this you must make sure that the customer actually receives the call back or all credibility will be lost.

Internet Resources – If the caller wants product information, or other information available on the company website, you could offer that option to the caller. This way the caller can get their information when they want over the web. Another advantage of this is that the caller will be introduced to your web site where they can get their information in the future.

Offer to send information by mail, e-mail, or fax – If the caller needs information or forms, offer to send the information to the caller by any one of these methods. E-mail and fax are instant ways to get information into the hands of people almost immediately.

There may be other options available in certain circumstances. Whatever can be done to help a caller without placing them on hold should be offered. Generally, the more options available to a caller, the more likely they are to be satisfied with the result. Making it easy for the caller is what it's all about.

Taking Messages & Using Voicemail

Voicemail and messages are one important way for callers to leave information and get responses. It is a preferred method when compared to repeatedly calling back trying to reach a very hard to contact person.

There are pitfalls to voicemail and messages, however. First, this form of communication is extremely impersonal and frustrating to a caller who needs attention at that particular time. If the caller needs immediate attention, voicemail just does not fit the bill. How would you feel if you were having a heart attack and you called 911 and was told to leave a message and someone would get back to you within 24 hrs? Not a real appropriate option is it?

Some companies today use voicemail instead of additional personnel during busy periods of the day.

For example, if 5 phone people are need during busy periods each day but only 2 are need during other times, they might staff the department with 3 people and use voicemail for the spillover. The messages would then be returned during the slower periods. This is not a good practice but it still exists.

The single most important aspect of using voice mail effectively is to return phone calls in a timely manner. Returning phone calls quickly makes the callers feel good about the level of attention they are given as well as a feeling that you care about their needs. The opposite is also true. If you take long periods of time to return calls, it says to the callers "Your needs are not important to us." Generally speaking, the faster you respond, the better off you will be.

Voice mail greetings should identify the name of the person that you are leaving the message for as well as an expected time frame for a return call. If the person is out of the office for a few days, or on vacation, the greeting should let the caller know when they will return. If it is longer than a day or two, give the name of someone else that can help the caller in your absence.

HINT: If you are going to be out of the office for several days or weeks, add a day or two to your time out of the office to give yourself a chance to return messages. If you say you will return on Monday the 5th, callers will call you that day at 9 in the morning annoyed that you haven't called them back yet!

Some people will not realize that you returned to the office and had 57 messages waiting for you. Giving yourself an extra day or two will help you respond to everyone in a timely manner. Callers will never complain about getting a call back sooner than expected!

In your greeting, giving a time frame for a return call sets a level of expectations in the minds of your callers. Make sure that you can make your return calls within that timeframe. Failure to do that will have a negative effect in future dealings with this caller.

We all have times when things happen that prevent us from returning calls in a timely manner. We may have an emergency, get sick, or have an unforeseen thing come up. When this happens, always make your return calls as quickly as possible and offer an apology to your caller. Make the apology right after you identify yourself so that you diffuse any frustration and anger that may have developed in the mind of your caller.

There may be times when a caller will leave you a message that should have gone to someone else. When this occurs, you should do two things:

Transfer the message to the correct party – Make sure that the message goes to the correct person and ask them to respond to the caller as soon as possible.

Call the original caller and give them the updated information - Since the caller has your name as the person with whom they left the message, you should contact the caller and give them the name of the new person and tell them you asked that person to contact you as soon as possible. If that person is unavailable for a few days, let the caller know that also. Better they should know that instead of thinking that their message is being ignored.

Always make sure that every message gets returned in a timely manner and no request gets ignored or goes unanswered. If you cannot do this it is better to remove voicemail from your list of available options for your callers.

Ending A Call

When it comes time for a call to end, it is important that it end properly. The end of a call is where the customer refines their opinion and perception of their experience. The ending should provide closure and make sure that all the issues have been addressed and properly acted upon.

Closure is very important. All to often, one or more issues will unfortunately have been forgotten in the process. We may go to great lengths to resolve one issue while accidentally forgetting another. We do not do this intentionally; we just target all our efforts in one direction and become consumed with the task at hand. When this happens, everything else just falls by the wayside.

Ending a call should consist of several parts. They are:

Thank You

Make sure you take the time to thank the customer for calling. Make sure they are aware that you appreciate the opportunity to help the customer. Let them know you are there to help them.

Ask Them If There Is Anything Else You Can Do For Them

Ask the caller if there is anything else you can do for them. Review what has transpired and make sure to give them the opportunity to think of anything else that they might need. This increases the chances that nothing will be forgotten. Sometimes people feel uncomfortable asking for something else after they have been helped out in another matter. Asking the questions allows them the opportunity to easily ask for assistance in other matters.

Let The Caller Know How To Contact You In The Future

Another effective way to make the best of the situation is to let the caller know how to contact you in the future. By saying something like; "Remember, Mrs. Nelson, if you need anything else in the future, please make sure to call me at 555-6767. My name is Anne. I will be happy to help you." This will leave a very positive impression with the caller. It will also increase the likelihood that the caller will call back or purchase products for you in the future.

Ending The Call

When ending the call, make sure to leave the customer with a pleasant ending such as; "Have a nice day" or "Thank you for calling." This is a positive way to end a call and create a favorable impression.

As with all other parts of the conversation, the ending is an important part whose importance should not be overlooked. It is part of the overall experience that is intended to create positive impressions and address the needs of the caller. With practice, a good and proper ending becomes automatic. In the beginning make every effort to craft a proper and effective ending. As you start using it, you will begin doing it without thought or effort. It will become part of your "phone personality."

Just like other parts of phone skills, a company should strive to maintain a uniform way of ending calls. The wording does not have to be the same. In fact, each person should craft his or her own ending so it doesn't sound like a "canned" or insincere response. The ending should be individualized but still include all the parts mentioned in this chapter.

Call Waiting & Caller ID!

Call waiting and caller ID are two newer options that are becoming quite popular in both residential and business applications. Call waiting lets a person know when someone else is trying to call them while they are already on the phone. Caller ID lets a person know who is calling them when the phone rings. Their name and number shows up on a small screen on the phone.

Call Waiting

Call waiting lets a person know when another party is trying to contact them. The receiver will beep or make a sound when someone else is calling. The person can then place one person on hold and talk to the other person. This feature is important in the respect that a really important or emergency call can get through when the phone is in use. Without call waiting he result would be a busy signal when there is an urgent need to contact someone.

As with any feature, there are guidelines for its use. In order to avoid offending people we should use this feature only in certain situations. Just like stopping a conversation to accept a call on a cell phone, placing someone on hold to see who else is calling may also be considered rude. It is like saying to someone; "Hold on, this person may be more important or interesting than you."

Although you would never say that to someone, you actions are, in fact, saying just that. A good rule of thumb is to not answer the second call when you are involved I any kind of business call or meeting. An exception to this rule would be when you are waiting for an important call or a call that pertains to the conversation you are now having.

For example, you are having a conversation with an account regarding last quarter's sales figures. If you know your accounting department is going to call you with the latest figures, you may place the party on hold to take that call and get the updated information.

Another example would be if a member of your family was in trouble or involved in some kind or emergency. In a case like this, you would say something like this to the person you are currently talking to; "John, my daughter has been in labor and the baby is due any minute. That may be my wife o the other line. Just let me put you on hold for one minute." Unless the situation is so formal and important, no reasonable person would take exception to being placed on hold.

Call Waiting should not be used as way to make sure you take every call from friends, family, and other non-business people during working hours. It is a useful tool in making sure you are available to callers who have a need to speak with you. In this context it is a valuable tool. Just make sure you use it correctly.

Caller ID

Caller ID is a somewhat new feature over the last few years. This feature lets the person being called know who is one the other end of the phone. The person's phone number and name will appear on a display on the phone.

This is useful in identifying people who call and don't leave a number, people who make threatening or harassing phone calls, or people who refuse to identify themselves. This can be useful information. Keep in mind, however, that the opposite is also true. When you call a person, your company name will appear on their phone. Even a call that is not answered may be logged in the caller ID memory!

It is important to realize this because this means you can't tell a person that you tried to call but no one was home and you didn't want to leave a message. The person will know that your number was not on his ID log and will catch you in the lie!

It is possible to block your number from appearing on caller ID screens. This is available through the phone company at a charge. If you or your company has a valid reason for blocking this information, contact your local phone company.

Cell Phones!

If there is one advent of technology that has changed our everyday life it is the advent of the affordable cell phone. Just 10 years ago cell phones were cost prohibitive and extremely bulky and heavy. Now they can fit in the palm of your hand and cost just a few dollars a month! Because of this, more people have them and their use is increasing almost on a daily basis.

Along with this technology comes a change in the way we use phones for business. Cell phones, like any other device, can be used correctly or abused. We see examples of this everyday in our lives.

Who hasn't seen the person involved in a deep conversation at the checkout register, which prevents them from getting their plastic out to pay for their groceries? Or the person talking a mile a minute, while driving 60 miles an hour, and reading a map at the same time? The nest time you go out, look for examples like this. You'll be surprised how many you'll find.

If you routinely get calls from people over their cell phones, try and get a home number also for a call back. Cell phones offer greatly increased availability but it may do you no good to reach someone during a movie or dinner. For example, if you need information that the person has at home, contacting them at the supermarket will serve no useful purpose. Always try to get a home number for callbacks.

Be careful giving out cell phone numbers of employees. Make sure you know the policy of the company regarding this. If no such policy does exist, it is good practice to ask each person and get his or her preference.

The reason for this is that cell phones obliterate one's privacy. No longer are callers restricted to office hours to call someone. They can call weekends, evenings, even on Christmas Day! Unless an occupation requires access 24 hours a day (physician, fire fighter, policeman, etc), you should be careful giving out numbers to callers without permission. If you are not sure what to do, always make your judgment on the safe side. Tell the caller you will contact the person and have them return the call as soon as possible. While this may not make the customers happy, it does maintain the privacy of the person involved.

Accepting Calls On Cell Phones

Another activity that people view as being very rude is answering a cell phone during a meeting or conversation with someone else.

When you are talking to someone and stop the conversation to take a cell call, what you are saying to that person is "What you are saying is not that important to me right now. Wait until I am done with this other person." If someone were to actually say that to you, how do you think this would make you feel? Chances are, not very good. Yet there are a lot of people who do this very thing day after day!

I have been in meeting where people actually leave the meeting to answer a cell phone! These are not important calls that require action but rather ordinary calls! I even had a person answer a cell phone during a funeral service!!! There is a time and place for everything.

A good rule of thumb is to turn your phone off, or set it to silent mode, during any meeting. The only exception would be if you were waiting for a call pertaining to that particular meeting. If you are talking to someone, do not halt that conversation to speak to someone else. It is rude, it's insulting, and it's demeaning. However you say it, it's just wrong! I tell people working for me that they should never interrupt a meeting or conversation to answer their cell. I make it clear that this is the policy. If you are expecting an important call, tailor you voicemail message accordingly and give the caller a timeframe when they can expect a call back.

When using your cell phone to make calls, make sure you do so in a safe and proper manner.

Trying to dial while driving (illegal in some areas unless hands free phones are used) is not a smart idea. It interferes with keeping your eye on the road. It also should prohibit you from writing down information or focusing on operating a motor vehicle! If you must talk to someone while driving, try and pull off to a rest area or other place where you can concentrate.

Keep in mind also that the people in the supermarket do not care why XYZ Corporation needs your Model 123 Server units. They just want you to pay and let the next person on line get served. People in a movie theatre also do not want to listen to you close a sale or talk to your Aunt Edna about her arthritis! Lastly, if I'm paying good money for a steak dinner, I shouldn't have to listen to someone talk about reaching a sales quota or what happened at the bar last night. This is also rude and inconsiderate.

Cell phones, like speakerphones, do not offer much of a degree of privacy. Instead, they act like an intrusion or distraction to the people around them and should be used with respect to those around you. Keep in mind that, no matter how important you think you are, your conversations are of little or no interest to the general public. Keep that in mind and use your cell accordingly.

Using The Telephone
As a Sales Tool!

Disclaimer: This publication is designed to provide information based on the importance of creating a positive impression of a company or individual. It is NOT designed to provide information on telemarketing skills or other similar activities. We are dealing only with providing excellent customer service to our callers and customers.

The telephone can be a great sales tool. You can make maybe 20 calls in an hour to 20 different businesses or customers. If you had to travel to each location, you might only be able to get to 1 or 2 of those people in the same time frame. It also allows you to contact people for considerable less money. Because of this, some companies use the telephone to gather leads and create sales. If you or your company does this, there are a few things you should be aware of.

Do Not Call At Inconvenient Times!

Have you ever wondered why you get so many calls at dinnertime? You get those calls because research has determined that more people will be at home during the hours of say, 5 pm to 7 pm. Because more people tend to be home, the companies have a far greater chance of actually talking with someone rather than leaving a message or just abandoning a call. While this is good for actually being able to talk to someone, it can be bad for the company.

Interrupting a family's dinner is not a positive thing to do. Most people who answer the phone during their diner are not going to be happy talking to a telemarketer. Even if they are interested in what you have to say, they will not be happy to let their dinner get cold while you make their sales pitch. Neither one of these factors is a positive for you or your company.

I would suggest you try to make your calls at a more convenient time. Later on in the evening (but not too late for the people that go to bed early!) may give you a good connection rate while not interrupting mealtime. Remember that we want to create a positive feeling in the mind of our customers. Keeping their interests and feelings in mind will help us to do that.

Do Not Bombard People With Repeated Calls!

Another thing most people do not like at all is repeated phone calls from the same company.

Think about how you felt when you received the 50th phone call from Harry's Chimney Sweeps. Were you thrilled to hear from them again? More likely you would file their name in your "Do not call them when we do need a chimney sweeping in the future" file. Bombarding people with call after call damages your reputation and 'cheapens" your image. Keep track of when you call people and make sure a sufficient time frame goes by before you call them again.

If They Ask You To Stop Calling, STOP!

Sometimes when you call a person, they will ask you not to call again. If this happens, your system should have a way of removing that person's phone number from the calling list. This should be done for two reasons. First, it shows respect for the person you called, which will help you to avoid creating a negative impression. Secondly, and more important, it may be illegal to keep calling that customer and may result in a fine!

In some areas, there is something called a "Do Not Call" list. This list contains names and numbers of people who have registered their dislike for marketing calls and indicated that they do not wish to receive any more of these calls. If you should keep calling someone who is on this list, you could wind up paying a hefty fine and some poor publicity.

People HATE Automated Sales Messages!

People as a rule cannot stand those annoying automated and pre-recorded sales messages. More common around election time, these messages are impersonal and do not inspire confidence. Most people place them on the same level as Internet E-mail "SPAM"!

One very annoying part of some of these messages is that the system does not release the phone line after a person hangs up. The line stays connected until the message is finished! If the message is 3 minutes long, then the phone line is "held captive" for the 3 minutes! If the person hangs up and then tries to make a call a few seconds later, they still hear the message when they lift the receiver! This drives people crazy!

While I do not believe there is a case where this happened, I would be afraid that using this kind of system might prevent someone from making a very important call. Suppose someone was having trouble breathing and the phone rang with one of these messages. The people would not be able to call for medical help until the message finished! How do you think the homeowner would feel about your company now?

If you do feel that automated messages are a good fit for your company, please try to use a system that releases the line whenever the called person hangs up the phone. It will not cost you sales and it will save you a lot of negative feelings.

Whatever You Decide To Do, Keep Your Callers In Mind!

A good rule of thumb would be to put yourself in the place of the customer when thinking about your approach regarding telemarketing. Try to tailor your message and calling times to fit the needs and lifestyle of the people you are calling. This will increase your response rate and minimize some of the negatives that usually are associated with this type of activity.

If you use a pre-recorded message, try to use one that you would feel comfortable reading to a live person on the other end of the phone. Try to keep the message short and o the point. You are using this message to create interest and obtain a lead not close a sale. Keep that in mind when designing your message.

I firmly believe in "taking the high road" whenever you are dealing with people. Your long-term relationship with your customers and callers are more important than the quick buck made from a single sale today. Your reputation is something that may take years to create and just minutes to destroy. Be very careful when designing your telemarketing program.

Developing Your Telephone Skills!

The key to changing any behavior, or learning a new skill, is to break down the act or behavior into small pieces and change one small thing at a time until the change is complete. Trying to change too quickly requires too much concentration and effort and will likely result in failure.

If you are learning a new position, you know how daunting a challenge can be. You start out knowing nothing and are faced with pages of rules to learn, procedures to follow, and information to commit to memory. Your first days on the job are stressful and not very productive.

My suggestion is to determine which skills you will use most often and work on those first. Practice and develop your greeting until your feel comfortable. By doing something until you feel comfortable will allow you to then forget about that task and concentrate on something new. Treat each skill as a building block on which to add new skills later.

Try and define the most basic things you have to do. Learn those things and commit them to memory. Do this until they become automatic for you and require no thought or effort. When you have reached that point you can add other more specific skills to what you have already learned.

For example, think about when you were little and learning to ride a bike. First you would sit on the bike and practice steering and reaching the pedals. Then you would ride while someone held the bike and ran with you. When you got comfortable with that, the person would let go but still run next to you. Then, you would ride solo. It was a natural progression of skills that you built upon until you learned the whole procedure.

The same process is used in learning how to drive, play a musical instrument, or use tools. Start with the basics and work towards more complicated things when you are ready. This has been proven to be the most effective and lasting way to learn new skills and develop new talents.

Use Resources Around You!

If there are others in similar positions with you, ask them how to do certain things. These people have experience in dealing with the tasks and skills that you need to learn. They can drastically reduce the time required to learn things and become proficient. They can tell you what to do and what not to do.

They can help you learn from mistakes that they had made. This will save you time and effort.

It is important that you don't feel you have to re-invent the wheel. It is perfectly all right to listen to others to find out what works and what doesn't. Don't fall into the trap of thinking that everything you are told is right for you. What worked for one person may not work for another. Just as people are different, so are work habits and personalities. You may not be able to talk and act like the others in your group. Because of this, you may have to modify your approach. This is perfectly normal and should be part of your approach.

Listen to others and keep an open mind. Use what works for you and discard what doesn't work. The focus should be only on doing what works for you and what helps you learn faster, more easily, and more effectively.

Conclusion

Always remember that your voice over the phone is the only thing your callers can use to base their opinions and make judgments on. They can't see you or your product or see what kind of facilities you work in. They can only hear what you are saying and how you are saying it.

Know how your particular phone system works and know how to use all the features you will use during your time on the phone. Make sure you present a calm and positive demeanor during your conversation and make sure you treat each and every caller with the respect they deserve.

Speak using only positive comments, words, and phrases. Let your callers know what you can do to help them and do not offer excuses as to why you cant do something. Let them know how you can help them. Don't dwell on what you can't do.

Take the lead during the conversation and make the caller feel important.

Let them know you appreciate their calls and thank them for the opportunity to be of service to them.

Never view a caller as a distraction or inconvenience. Spend the time required to help them with whatever their needs may be at that time. Be the person that's there for them to vent their frustrations. Let them talk until they calm down. Listen carefully to what they say and develop a plan to address their concerns.

Make callers part of the process and solicit their opinions. Very often they will ask for less than what you were going to offer. Let them tell you what they would like to see happen. Then negotiate what you feel is fair.

Always take the time to listen. Listen to what the caller is saying and what they are not saying. Try and read between the lines to see what the problem really is.

Keep the customer informed every step of the way. If you are transferring the caller, let them know the name of whom you are transferring them to and the number. Never leave a caller hanging without letting them know what is going on.

Always treat everyone with respect. That goes for off the phone too!

For more information on Customer Service Training, please go to:

http://www.infowhse.com

www.ingramcontent.com/pod-product-compliance
Lightning Source LLC
Chambersburg PA
CBHW050821150526
45103CB00022B/302